RITUALS

RITUALS

Kiriti Sengupta

HAWAKAL

Poems and other texts illustrated by
Partha Pratim Das

Published by Hawakal Publishers, 185, Kali Temple Road, Nimta,
Calcutta 700049, India.
Website: www.hawakal.com
Contact: info@hawakal.com

First edition: April, 2019
Printed and bound at S. P. Communications, Kolkata

ISBN-13: 978-93-87883-52-9
Price: INR 300.00 | USD 10.99

To the *Baul*s

Embracing Rituals

How much does ritual depend on nature? In this slim volume, poet Kiriti Sengupta explores the boundary between human nature and the world of Nature. He also muses on the concept of Indian identity and the distinct relationship a person of India has with the remainder of the world.

In *"Kalprivksha,"* Sengupta writes these eloquent lines of the divine tree: *"Grounded on / earth and its evil, prepares them for prayers."* Such verses carry the meditations from the natural world into the world of supernatural immediacy. What the lines appear to say is that evil itself, while not explicable in human terms, exists to direct our consciousness to the world of God. God must have known we would not rely much on His counsel if nothing existed to require redemption. In response to this question of theodicy, the young Anne Frank wrote these lines in her diary, "It's difficult in times like these: ideals, dreams and cherished hopes rise within us, only to be crushed by grim reality. It's a wonder I haven't abandoned all my ideals, they seem so absurd and impractical. Yet I cling to them because I still believe, in spite of everything, that people are truly good at heart." Frank kept her hopes in humanity, knowing that despite the evil we enact we are still children of a benevolent power. In issue four of *Dialogos* Richard W. Kropf writes, "But just suppose that *evolution*, as it is commonly understood, both on the inorganic but even more on the organic level, might be the *only* way that God 'creates' or indeed even *can* create. Thus, as the evidence indicates, the Creator seems to have had to begin with the disordered state of energy in which the universe appears at its very beginning. And then suppose, in addition, that the aim or goal for creation is the eventual appearance of intelligent, free creatures, beings who, to some extent, are able to share God's own attributes."

Anne Frank and Richard Kropf are wrestling with the same theological doubts. Ritual, properly understood, signifies gratitude and is rooted in the habitual nature of the human organism. In a state of nature, we are feeble creatures subject to flux and irrational occurrences that breed fear and awe into our composition. This state could be called "reverence" and it is shared by religious authorities, scientists, and the average person alike. Albert Einstein wrote in a letter known as the "God letter" that "The word God is for me nothing more than the expression and product of human weakness." However, he also wrote to the Hungarian mathematician Cornelius Lanczos, "What I see in Nature is a magnificent structure that we can comprehend only very imperfectly, and that must fill a thinking person with a feeling of 'humility.' This is a genuinely religious feeling that has nothing to do with mysticism."

The poem "After the Book Fair" negotiates a different kind of ritual, one of passing. After the fair, there is an inevitable sigh of relief and period of cleaning up. Rejuvenation is implied in the lines, *"From the shelves new hope will follow / the merchandise."* After days of selling and promoting, the authors and publishers store their books to launch their sales at another place and time. The strangeness in the poem is its implication that everyday affairs are a kind of ritual containing elements of redemption, hope, and finality.

The reader returns to the question of Indian identity in the poem "Faith" as Sengupta outlines particular rituals, *"Rituals do not add to our credos."* What is the proposition here? National identity is larger than religion and ritual. So we are tossed to our backs on the question of the importance of ritual. What makes ritual important and necessary in human life? How exactly does it define us and our relationship with the world?

The final poem "Exhibition" gives us startling wake-up call in true Ozymandias fashion. Sengupta's "traveler from an antique land" is himself, observing the ancient exhibits in a museum. He makes one strange observation. The various artifacts are missing their noses! The poet then playfully teases the historical pride of man, *"Nature made the nasal frame fragile. / How do they breathe the vain air?"*

These poems in a surprisingly original way remind us of the folly of human arrogance, the beauty of the historical circumstance in which we are situated, the impermanence and grandeur of Nature, and the need we humans have in our mortality to create habit from a fear of death, destruction, and chaos in order that we can praise life's gravity and uniqueness before the vastness of its being.

Rituals unifies many aspects of human life in one bold cry of vexation. The poet remains agnostic about his discoveries and dances quizzically throughout his words as if to sustain his curiosity. Sengupta, in this new collection of both personal meditations and social commentary, proposes to move his work into new territory. His previous writings have spoken of tradition, family, culture, solitude, Nature, and womanhood with a curiosity and sense of awe. This collection carries that mission forward. After *Solitary Stillness*, these meditations will appear less solitary and meditative. Rather, they embrace a universal human paradigm. Sengupta discovers ways to approach this paradigm with clarity and compassion. He both accepts and distances himself from human evil while expressing his gratitude toward the "infinite jest" that composes life. His reflections on the gifts that make his life wonder-filled bring us closer to the heart of this man of bestselling poetry.

It is this aspect of *Rituals* I find most satisfying to embrace. We face a man in his reflections and see ourselves in his personal meditation. He does not shy to make this line of inquiry about us, the people. All readers of this collection will find satisfaction in discovering their own rituals.

Dustin Pickering
Jan 14, 2019
Houston, Texas, USA

Acknowledgements

It's Dustin Pickering who has named the collection. Pickering has also written the foreword to *Rituals*. He deserves the first note of thanks.

I'm grateful to everyone who has helped *Rituals* in more than one way: Sanjeev Sethi, Mosarrap Hossain Khan (editor, *Cafe Dissensus*), Bitan Chakraborty (founder, *Hawakal*), Pinaki De (cover designer), Partha Pratim Das (illustrator), Bhaswati (wife), and Aishikk (son).

I'm thankful to the journals/magazines that have published a few poems included in this collection: *Oddball Magazine, Noble/Gas Qtrly, The Florida Review Online (Aquifer), The Common, Mad Swirl, Headway Quarterly, The Mark Literary Review, Moria Online, Juke Joint Magazine, Setu Bilingual,* etc.

Contents

Comeback

I return after a year. The room is full of dust, the floor smeared with thick silt; the mirror on the wall is glued to ripped paint, and it deceives. Several prominent lips on cups and plates...cigarette butts stick out from the water jar...the filth radiates intimate odor. My tired eyes uncover the kohl of night, while my glasses spot tears. The fruit-platter was in the storeroom — the leftovers ache...did someone split the cord of the earphone?

The Resurrection

Slumber unfolds its arms as it wakes up. The tiny particles scattered in the air absorb the sunlight; they seem to be delighted and drone the song of liberation. Sleep is now conscious like the attraction between mother and her new-born.

Flawlessly arranged, the room is ready for hard work and is not yet marked by fatigue. At a distance, the mother awaits her demonstration in sweat and grime.

On the Richter Scale

i

It's drizzling since cockcrow. It won't stop. They name it the hallmark of the season. Winter precipitates. 4 on the Richter scale sits comfortably on the human body. A scattered crowd walks on the street. Roadside lamps romance with their acrylic veneers. Doused Banyan trees await desiccation. West side of the footpath marks the ghettos. Here the residues burn. Frozen limbs budge. Numb nerves wish to whistle.

ii

Fleeing the house and leaving the doors ajar. Is it perversion or fallacy? To amble solitary in winter is amusing. It provides solace for some time. Smoke does not arise as the mouth opens. Tiny crystals of ice accumulate along the crease. They melt as the nip recedes, barring a hint of steam. An aberration? No trace of forgotten ventilators, the fumes swirl to ascend. The scale marks 5. Does vapor perspire?

iii

A seven-year-old canvas invites dust bunnies. Mopping whitens it; gray patches lurk in the brightness. It looks at the artist, Desolation, who paints fresh water-colors. The cloth blushes. It absorbs all the cuddles. The elbow hits and makes it pale. The veil dissolves. A mirror bathes in glassy water to reflect light. The sea longs for a rendezvous. Desolation stands still. The Richter scale fails to respond.

Appraisal

1

Timing is crucial, to say the least.
Do you consider Nature baffling?

We can certainly look up to the sun
at dawn and dusk, or when it rains.

2

Patrons do not frequent ageing
accolades anymore. In a pristine
white bed, they have been resting
for ages. Several vases hold roses
on the bedside table, but refuse
to scent the décor. The flowers aren't dry;
they haven't shed petals either.

An appraiser is called out to rouse
commendation.

When God is a Woman

How many householders meet in
a whorehouse?

How many *mujra*s dwell in a *kotha*?

How many neonates hew to a bordello?

Like her admirers
God is silent.
In her sinews
hides a hint of soil
from the yard of courtesans.

Accommodation

Rain or moisture,
what do ferns long for?

Downpour evicts roots,
dampness helps them
settle on the rocks.

Male

I find myself connected
when my child says *Baba*.

Moments of intimacy surface
when my wife wants me to listen.

Mother makes sense
when she calls me son.

Performing the last rites
adds to the legacy.

The Expectant Mother

She lies supine.
Close to her chest she holds
a greased mango leaf,
blazed to kohl. Her eyes
whist like a whisper.

She stretches her hands
to douse the sky
with blood and water.

Tradition

I have no choice but to listen
to the same words again and again.
Neither am I aware of consequences.
It is not cerebral but sensory.

Customs are like meditation —
worthy of unhurried contemplation.
Practice adds to their maturity,
I know servitude is congenital.

The Blues

The door is closed.
It is difficult to remember when
light entered the guardhouse.
In this heavy air
how does one breathe?

As the gate opens wide
I see a run for pleasure.
Horizon marks salvation.

Not in allegories,
but in eyes, lust flickers!

In extreme hunger,
how does one understand economy?
Wants mask the subconscious.

Nascence

In a blanket of butter
there is more stillness than action.
There is no sound of awakening.
Are words sleeping?

In the zero hour
you are in my eyes.
Why am I weary?

Expressions know denial.
Wellspring, are you awake?

Kalpavriksha

Who says it is fetched from Heaven?
Do the gods need it to fulfill a wish?

Trees are girdled by threads of trust. They
evolve to be imperturbable. Grounded on
earth and its evil, prepares them for prayers.

Note: *Kalpavriksha*, also known as *Kalpataru*,
is a wish-fulfilling divine tree in Hindu mythology.

Images

What does it take
to look like an Indian?
A *saree, dhoti,*
or a *diya* for *ārtī?*

Sit on the floor cross-legged,
better if you can do the half-lotus.
Forget the angle your hindlimbs
form in a plane.
With closed eyes
let your index finger meet the first digit,
and others stretch outward.
Keep your smile.

India meditates across the map,
guided or otherwise, sometimes
endorsing a pair of faded jeans.

Notes: *ārtī* (also spelled aarti/arati) is a Hindu religious ritual of worship in which light (usually from a flame) is offered to one or more deities. *Diya* is a lamp used in religious affairs.

Timings

It's difficult to sever amity
even if it fails.
A new friend splits the bond
faster.

Why do we hold stars
responsible for the rift?
Once in a while
it is crucial to get cornered.

That's when
I touch
the fiber of camaraderie.

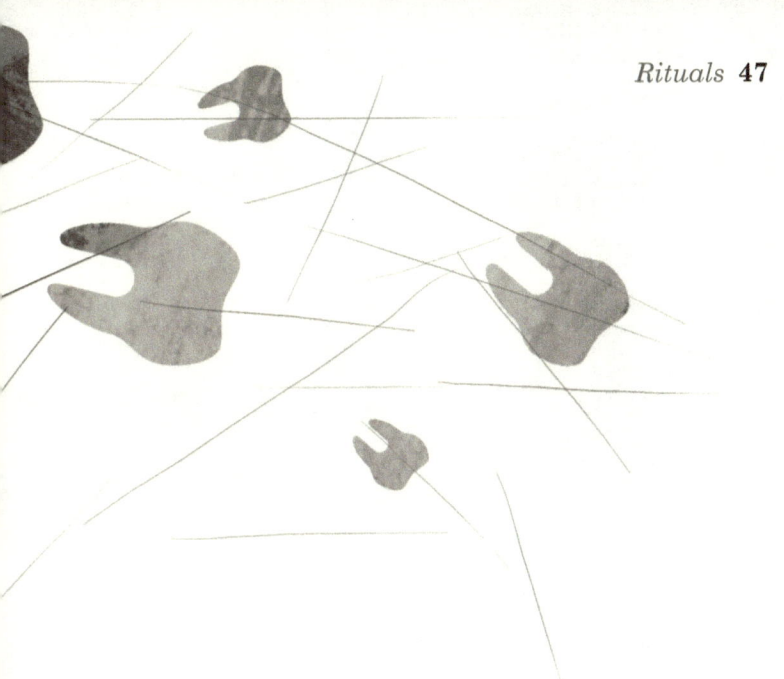

Dentures

I prefer patients who are edentulous. I dread
a tooth will wrangle my expertise, and I'll fail
to make an impression.

Religion

The shirt I bought waives promises.
It attracts stains, odors, and crumples
briskly. The salesman had insisted,
We treat cotton to produce
fine fabric.

Isn't propensity native? It refutes
mutation.

From Being Late in Calcutta

As soon as you mark me
I'll talk about events
that guide me to the records
you maintain.

I'd say crowded buses invite passengers
from unscheduled halts.
I'd emphasize the number of speed-breakers on road,
and their poor performance in preventing accidents.

I'd tell you trains run late.
Signals are laggy between stations.
I won't forget to mention how
a sudden protest
makes the train stand still for hours.

I'd discuss about the day I reported late,
owing to instantaneous suspension
of underground train services
as a man killed himself on the railway lane.

I'd ask you to remember why I came late the other day.

If you can recall,
I had indigestion despite eating at home.
I blamed farmers for sprinkling pesticides on crops.
I pointed at my salary that failed to buy organic veggies.

And then,
I'd invariably argue about maintenance and population.

I'd appreciate China, one-child policy, and their claim on
how the government prevented four hundred million births.
And how India thrives on the revenues earned
from selling nicotine and condoms.

I'll explore other issues
the next time I reach late.

Gravity

The aircraft takes off.
First officer alerts,
The dismal climate may cause turbulence.

Upheavals follow air-pockets.

My scared son grips the armrests.
I comfort him, *Relax! Bumps help us
realize the earth.*

Patience

I advise my part-time assistant
not to quit his day job and
ignore all coercions.
He should calm his nerves.

I speak of the banyan tree
stemming from the exterior cornice.
Roots penetrate concrete
until they are excised.

The Stepwell

Kalapani insinuates servitude for a lifetime.

In the premises of *Purana Qila*
the *baoli* is alive.

Eighty-nine stairs down
water is yet to scour the shine.
It awaits liberation.

Note: A stepwell is called *baoli*, regionally.

Observance

1
Visitors, who checked
in to see my father post-surgery,
appeared stressed.
After his discharge several came home.
Eyes moistened, they wished him Godspeed.
All of us except *Baba* knew...
Ma informed him months later.

No one pays a call anymore.
Three decades....

2

Tittle-tattle halts.
The mother waves a goodbye
as the school bus sets off.

3

Blame it on the state of mind.
Doted on as daughter, she
is the one I lust after. Thriving
on myths we build littoral
abodes for Lord *Shiva* along-
side the sacred *Ganga*.

Notes: *Shiva* is depicted in Hindu iconography as *Gangadhara*, the 'Bearer of the *Ganga*,' with *Ganga*, shown as spout of water, rising from his hair. *Shiva-Ganga* relationship is both perpetual and intimate. There are instances where *Ganga* has been considered *Shiva's* daughter.

4

Will this strategy work? I'm writing on menstruation, pregnancy and motherhood.

Menstrual blood is no different from the one the heart pumps. It is red, sticky and has a peculiar odor to it. That it is considered unholy in tribal setups is unscientific. Goddesses bleed and so does the gentle sex.

Pregnancy and motherhood are inseparable. Childlessness finds therapies and centers endorsing Tagore on display: *Amar hiyar majhe lukiyechile... (you hid inside my heart...).* Baby bumps foster designer labels. In the age of mental parenthood one may not conceive, deliver, or adopt to be called a mother.

I witness this from a distance. Does proximity help in faithful depiction?

Y-Gene

My friends were aware of the wish I nurtured.
If I had a daughter,
I would name her *Srividya*!
I was not influenced by any actor.
Our prayer room hosted a dazzling
crystal *Sri Yantra* on the holy altar.

My wife's desires were girly too.
She wished to drape her daughter
in frilly dresses.
She had plans to find her girl
a groom in clover, so my wife could
live comfortably! Prior to her labor,
my mother-in-law keenly observed
my wife's navel, *Come on, it's a boy*!
It was a boy, a cute little one
of two and a half kilos.

To take care of the borderline weight,
special supplements were arranged.
My wife looked proudly bright.
We worshiped the *Narayana*
right after the holy bath.

My son is at school.
It's a co-education convent.
After school he tells his mother,
Girls sit on the left side.

Screenplay

Death suggests how fruitless
it is to hold a grudge.
Life has ways to
recommence the soliloquy.

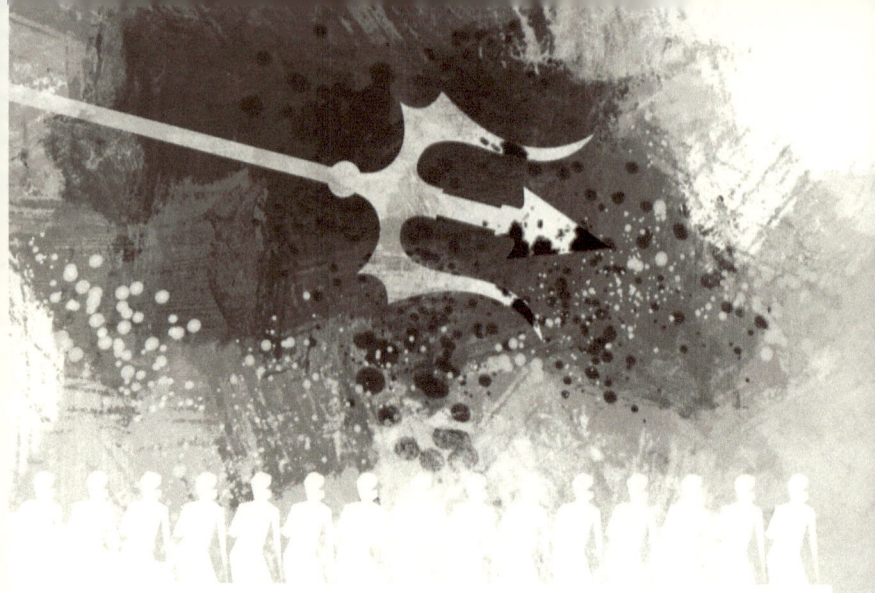

The Untold Saga

It took two hands
to kill *Mahishasura*.

Trishula was used
to destroy the demon.

Autumn accompanies
your ten-arm-avatar.

Like many women
you followed the husband.

You emerged from the gods.
You had several weapons!

The fiend was considered invincible.
You won the battle but did not claim the bounty.

That you are worshiped in earth
gave no relief to gasping *Nirbhaya*.

She was scourged by scoundrels
who dug into her body parts.

She followed death
thus could not create an epic.

Notes: *Nirbhaya* died from fatal injuries following gang-rape in Delhi in 2012. *Mahishasura* is a Sanskrit word composed of *Mahisha* (buffalo) and *Asura* (demon), indicating *buffalo demon*. As demon, *Mahishasura* waged war against the gods. He was ultimately killed by *Durga*. It is an important symbolic legend in Hindu mythology, particularly *Shaktism*. The legendary battle of *Mahishasura* as evil and *Durga* as good is narrated in many parts of South Asian and Southeast Asian Hindu temples, monuments and texts such as the *Devi Mahatmya*. *Trishula* is a trident, commonly used as the principal symbols in Hinduism and Buddhism. It is wielded by the god *Shiva*. *Durga* also holds a *trishula*, as one of her many weapons.

The Unclad God

There was a time I wanted to see
naked people.

Women — for obvious reasons.

Nude men affected me in many ways.
Every time I saw them
I became conscious of myself
followed by a comparative check.
If mine was shorter
I'd run to my workspace
and read a memo to myself.
It said size had nothing to do
with female orgasm.

Bare men reminded me
of my unkempt body hair,
how I had to trim and oil
to make it healthier.

I don't look at unveiled people anymore.
It is either my age or hormones.
I now look beyond the flesh, bone and keratin.

I've been told
the finer body dwells undressed.

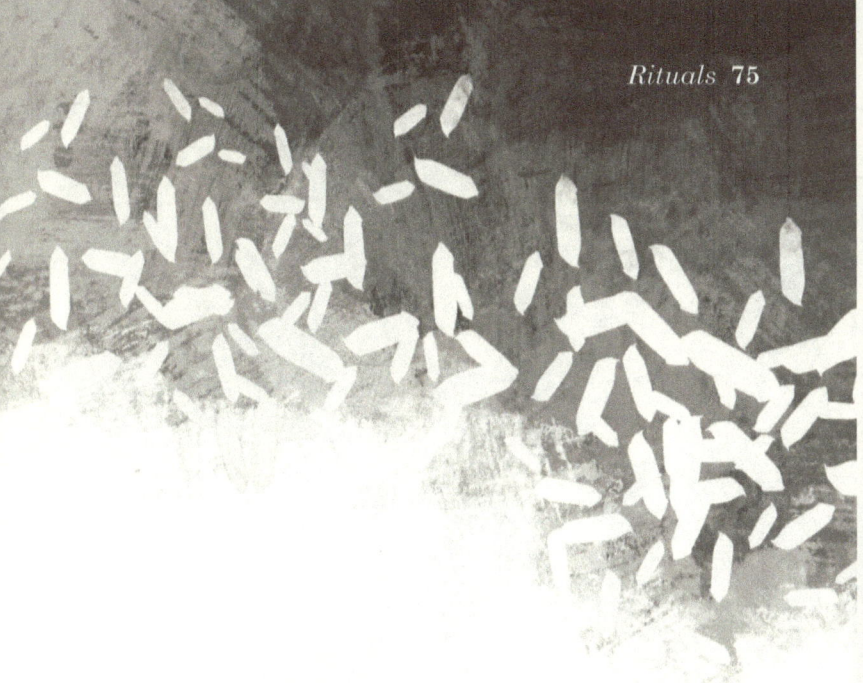

Promising Griefs

Neither the plough
nor the bankrupt farmer know
whether the earth will receive
optimum water.

Consider the rice seed—
Not sure if it will rejoice
sprouting into a plant
that will invariably die
to give us food for life.

Anyday

"If wishes were horses, beggars would ride."

Should I stop daydreaming? With open eyes I see events happen the way I want them to occur. They don't make me sweat, nor do they allow me to waste money I've been spending on movies. Unlike cinemas they hardly create an atmosphere of make-believe. Daydreams are unconventional. I paint them in all colors and emerge as champion. It's always a win-win situation that cannot be achieved in trance. I'm not Lord *Shiva*; marijuana doesn't help me envision aspirations in daylight. Daydreams allow monologues, design smiles on my lips. Blessed are the souls who daydream, for every moon has its share of nightmares.

The moments of harboring angst don't contribute to my reveries. They are regular leftovers of grim humors the dusk writes across the world of faeries.

A Place Like Home

Lights turned off,
three glasses retire
as the bar closes.
The first stands upright,
the other upside down,
another lies horizontal.

For last few hours
the crystals held liquor,
ice, scent and comfort.
They also witnessed
eyes that spoke volumes
while lashes refused
to flutter.

The pub reopens
the next day
to the riff of unrest.

The Season

What would I write to my wife on our sixteenth marriage anniversary?

Do I write how tender she used to be back in 2001? Do I thank her for being my partner for all these years? Or, do I express my gratitude for making me a father from a man?

I know I can't talk about her graceful ageing plans, for they will require her age to be acknowledged in the first place. I'm sure she won't be happy if I say, *Your lips lack luster*. My wife won't accept my advice for employing salon services; she does not seek suggestions anymore.

I'll rather compliment on flaunting those grey hairs I fondly call her silver lining. The rest of her black mane is yet to burn in the lightning flashes in the rain. For, mine is a world of the waters where time fails to reason and clouds gather time and again.

Jesus

How would a husband look in the eyes of his wife whose four-year-old daughter has been sexually abused by a male teacher in the school where she goes to play and learn?

O teacher, how would you palpate the anatomy of your wife, I'll bet, only to raise a complaint on her chastity?

But then, it's the world at large that believes in sex and how it spices up life or love, to be honest!

Note: A four-year-old girl was allegedly abused in GD Birla School in Calcutta on November 30, 2017.

The Heights

I've often heard people talking about how dwarfed they feel when they approach the mountains. So gigantic, they bewilder people to the extent that they find their mortal manifestations too insignificant to match the vastness of Nature. Having spent a decade in Siliguri, now a city on the foothills of the Himalayas, I remember its largest bus terminus that had been named after Tenzing Norgey, one of the two mountaineers to first reach the summit of Mount Everest. I think the bus depot, popularly called Junction, continues to send positive vibrations to travelers who intend to negotiate in every possible way the challenges Nature poses to keep her mysteries wrapped.

We came across a few plateaus on a recent trip to Darjeeling. As we got off the cab at Kurseong, Partha urged me, *Here it is difficult to comprehend the height, as if we are standing on the plain land.* I quickly replied: *The rise overwhelms the cliff. No matter how tall we stand, the hills accost our ascent at the pits and precipice!*

Anam weds Azhar

The wedding card looked gorgeous.
Younus, a friend, was full of praise for the
velvety feel, especially the golden letters
engraved on its maroon surface.

Recently we met over a lavish lunch, and
I got a chance to look at the invite.
Younus was justifiably right.
The invitation read:
Anam Weds Azhar

I was prompt to point at the line,
and asked whether the names
should have appeared in the reverse order.

In the course of nikah *the bride is asked first*
whether she willingly accepts the groom,
quipped his wife.

Sridevi

Your name hints at a goddess.
You endorse strength of will to the extent
that humans transform into snakes
and vice versa!

I wish you had taken away
all the venoms when you left.

Note: Reflecting on *Nagina,* a Hindi blockbuster, at the untimely demise of legendary Sridevi on Feb 24, 2018.

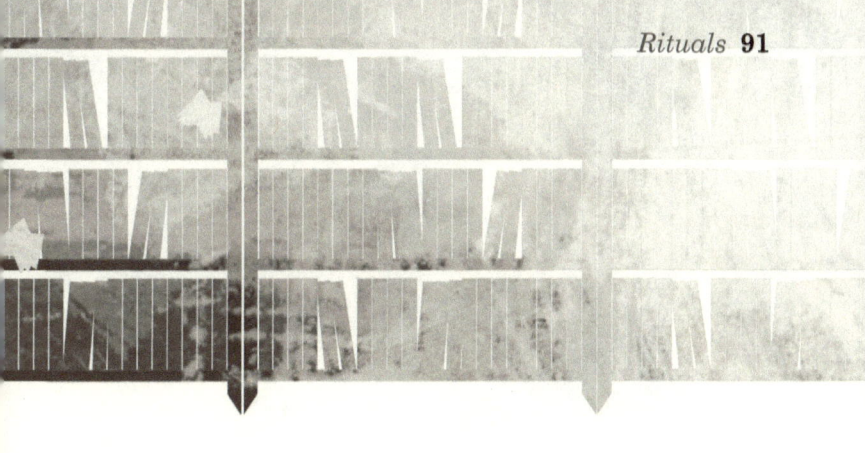

After The Book Fair

Their premises won't attract readers
anymore. Publishers, sellers, and a handful
of authors will spend hours in packing
books and goods unsold. From the shelves
new hope will follow the merchandise.
Apprehensions too will fill spaces in
the packs. A sense of relief prevails
over bargains.

Masala Muri

Ginger slices do not titillate
my taste-buds again.

The tangy golden of mustard oil
does not tease my nostrils anymore.

Onions fail to dew my eyes now;
they were never kept in cold water
before *Baba* chopped them; while he got
his lenses damp, *Ma* had tears.

On every stormy Sunday
we invariably had power cuts,
and *Baba* cooked dinner for us all:

a moderate serving of *Muri* mixed with
onion, ginger and blobs of oil.

On such occasions we used to sit close,
facing each other we shared our stories;
from airing endless grievances on our barren
curriculum, the dialogues on the utility
of learning Sanskrit,
to refuting *Ma*'s advice on being courteous
even to strangers we would meet.

Our room shined in kerosene lamps!

Load-shedding no longer casts its spell;
the back-ups are prompt and steady
we order food ... the mobile app comes handy,
but *Muri* seldom makes it to our monthly grocery.

The next monsoon I wish to buy
a new lantern,
and I'll light it once in a while
to accompany the old snack
and fresh stories in our family.

Note: *Muri* is a traditional Bengali snack, otherwise
called puffed rice.

The Marriage

I'm happily flaunting my marital status
for ages. Seeing this earnest union
a friend probes the combination. I add to
his impressions: *It is the wife, who keeps
trust on the consortium.*

Faith

Rituals do not add to our credos.

Rakhi enlivens familial warmth
without religious fidelity. On
Eid *seviyan* is for all.

Patrons stand-up in multiplexes
when the national anthem is relayed.

Indianness precedes theology.

Exhibition

I think of effigies with fractured noses.

Statuettes of gods, goddesses, kings,
unmasked in museums. Does this take
a toll on their pride?

Nature made the nasal frame fragile.
How do they breathe the vain air?